Angel Food
Spiritual Revelations

Gwen Watkins

PublishAmerica
Baltimore

© 2003 by Gwen Watkins.
All rights reserved. No part of this book may be reproduced, stored in a retrieval system, or transmitted in any form or by any means without the prior written permission of the publishers, except by a reviewer who may quote brief passages in a review to be printed in a newspaper, magazine, or journal.

First printing

"Accentuate the Positive," words by Johnny Mercer, music by Harold Arlen (HARWIN Music Corporation, 1944).

ISBN: 1-59286-279-9
PUBLISHED BY PUBLISHAMERICA, LLLP
www.publishamerica.com
Baltimore

Printed in the United States of America

"Manna! The very word defined means 'What is it?'" It is the bread that sustained God's people on a daily basis: Angel Food.

You are gaining insight on the author of Angel Food, the woman, Gwen Watkins. I call her "Mom." She has compiled years of prayers for me and many, many others, into this book. Prayer is simply talking to God. I am so glad Mom talked to God for me. Especially when I found it hard to speak to Him for myself.

She still prays for me today. The fruit of my life is people. The seed began with a woman's prayers and is still watered today in the same manner.

Keep these little insights on your person and draw on them for strength; God knows she did.

Love you Mom, G. F.

> Pastor G. F. Watkins
> Powerhouse Christian Center
> Katy, Texas 77493

"Angel Food" will be some of the best food you will ever eat, authored by one of the nicest ladies you will ever meet! Gwen has spent much time on God's training ground and her love for others exceeds her love for herself. She honors me by calling me her spiritual mother.

> Charlotte Holt, poet, author and friend.

I would just like to say, "I think it is funny how people are not willing to give up their so called lives to obtain salvation, but after they become saved they completely regret the lives they were not willing to give up." By no means were the Watkins ever deprived of worldly food as we can attest by our physical statues, but Mom brought us a helpful serving of Angel Food on a daily basis, which developed our spiritual bodies.
Thanks Mom - You are my Hero.
Love Ya, Brent

> Brent Watkins, preacher and coach.
> Mabank, Texas

DEDICATION

To my earthly Father, Rev. Gustaphus Adolphus Garig, now abiding with our Heavenly Father. May this book be the fulfillment of his earthly dream to write.

To my mother, Maggie Mae Matthews Garig, who passed on to me her stubborn will to achieve.

To my Heavenly Father, God, who made me and all the plans for my life, who sent Jesus, His Son, as proof of His love for me.

And to my best Friend, the Holy Spirit, who gave me the words for this book. Then, in the Father's perfect time, revealed how it would be financed.

ACKNOWLEDGEMENTS

To Faith Hiller who first believed in me and my ability to write. She never told me why her mother named her Faith...how foolish of me to ask.

To my many friends who lovingly tolerate my eccentric desire to become something far above my natural ability. They are right. Only the Holy Spirit could accomplish this.

To Sandy Massey McBride, my college roommate, who reappeared in my life just when I needed her. Sandy, having experienced the power of the Holy Spirit in her own life, accepts my limitations, knowing God is in control.

To my one and only earthly husband Gayle, who taught me more about my Heavenly Husband (God), than he will ever know. Thanks, Gayle!

To my precious sons G.F. and Brent, who continue treating their mom with love and respect, when she attempts to share her 'far-out' ideas.

To my brother Bruce who gave me an updated computer to encourage the continuance of this book which I began many years ago.

And to my older brother Glenn, who has always been there for me.

Most of all, to my Heavenly Father, who had mercy on me and sent the third part of His three-part vitamin.

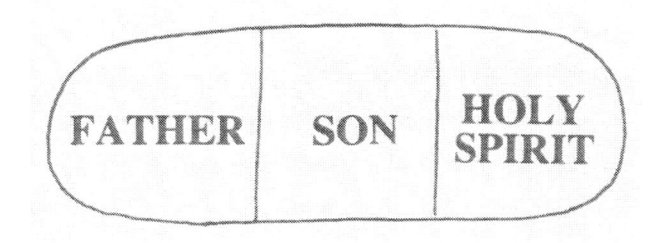

| FATHER | SON | HOLY SPIRIT |

CONTENTS

Foreword..11

I'm So Glad You Came..13

Manna, The Bread of Life...33

My Missing Dish..39

Desserts...53

More Desserts...59

FOREWORD

The information in this book is taken from what I now call "my honeymoon in the Holy Spirit."

I praise God that I wrote it as it happened. He has sped me so far and so fast since that first year. So far, I now realize that I know "nothing" compared to what there is yet to learn.

The truths I found through *Angel Food* remain as a foundation for me today. This book is for the reader who is curious about the Holy Spirit. One who has asked, "Lord, isn't there something more?"

Christians who have walked longer with the Holy Spirit may enjoy reminiscing. But, *Angel Food* is truly for the beginner.

As I continue to seek more knowledge and God's will, I understand the importance of this beginning. God was showing me the joy and fellowship He has to offer. I can't go back, yet I strive to constantly remain in the shadow of His loving presence.

This is just the beginning....

I'M SO GLAD YOU CAME

The door bell rings and I find myself running to answer it. Guess who it is? It's you! I'm so glad you accepted my invitation and came. A joy rushes through my body and spirit that's new in my life. I can hardly wait to share with you. Do you have time to listen? Oh, I hope so!

Seeing you standing by my door, I love you completely. You love me too because we're dear friends. How long has it been since we've seen each other? Too long! We must catch up...and we will, but God has something waiting for you. Because you're my friend and I love you so very much, I don't want you to spend another day of your life without the blessings you are about to receive.

God has prepared a special feast just for you. He's asked me to serve you bit-by-bit just as He served me.

Your meal is on the table.

COME IN!

As you enter the tastefully decorated living room with its cheery blues and golds, rays of sunshine filter through open windows, saturating the room with optimism. Scents of yeasty homemade bread create an aura of comfortable familiarity. Suddenly, a new aroma drifts through the room. No, it's more than one...it's many intoxicating fragrances. They appear to mingle, wafting in the space above your head, yet near enough to smell their exotic flavors. What are they? They are something new...something you've never tasted. As your curiosity grows, your spirit of adventure pushes you past me in your search.

Entering the dining room...there it is...the feast! It is absolutely the most beautiful array of delicacies you have ever seen; a variety of cool fruits, fresh vegetables, choice meats and decorative desserts of all kinds. Foods that look familiar, and those so extravagant only the wealthy can afford. A tablecloth and napkins of embroidered white linen, plates of gold, and the finest silverware enhance the richness of the moment. Ornate candles decorate each end of the long table, casting an iridescent and inviting glow. Somehow, it doesn't seem real.

Suddenly, you feel you've blustered into a place of holiness. You step back in awe as the scene appears more than you can fathom.

"Surely," you think, "this meal was prepared for someone else...not me."

As you slowly turn away, I place my hand on your shoulder and lead you gently to your place at the head of the table.

"But Gwen," you say, "I don't deserve this. I really don't."

"Oh yes you do," I answer. "Why else would God prepare it?"

"But it's so perfect...." you continue.

GOD IS PERFECT

Yes, the feast is perfect because God is perfect. Everything He does is perfect. He is supreme! There are no limits to God.

Do *you* honestly believe this? Many do not: even those who say they do. Would you like to believe this? I can show you how. Praise God! As He directed and fed me, He will direct and feed you.

God recognizes your needs, fears, and unquenchable hunger. You are not alone. Thousands like you, are looking for that missing ingredient to satisfy their appetite. Perhaps, like others, you are moving too fast to taste the food in front of you.

God has asked me to share with you some ancient recipes designed for your modern kitchen. These quick thoughts reach you 'on the run' in the hustle of your "fast foods world."

With one swift glance you capture a simple meaning from God's powerful Word; confident that not one of His Words will return void. Each will accomplish what it is sent to do.

*"So shall my word be that goeth forth out of my mouth;
it shall not return unto me void, but it shall accomplish
that which I please, and it shall prosper in the thing whereto
I sent it."*
Isaiah 55:ll (KJV)

As these recipes entice you into the Word and you allow them to become a way of life, they will produce fruit. You will experience immediate signs of improved health and vitality.

PROPER DIGESTION

Two ingredients are helpful to the proper digestion of Angel Food. The first is, that you are *truly* hungry. The hungrier you are, the more meaningful the message. Since your hunger led you to this book, it's obvious that you recognize your symptoms of spiritual malnutrition. No longer ignoring hunger pangs and the emptiness of your life; realizing that organic food is not enough, you show great wisdom in seeking 'something more.'

The second ingredient is that you *believe* the Bible is the "Inspired Word of God."

"All scripture is given by inspiration of God...."
2 Timothy 3:16 (KJV)

His Word is "Proof of the Pudding." You'll know the recipes work when you put them to use and see results.

I'm giving you a Recipe Card now so you can practice. (In case you need to prepare supper before completing this book.) Begin using it today.

From time to time, I will refer to words from the recipe cards and special bits of scripture by using *italic* letters. Add these as condiments to your established menu.

WHAT EXACTLY, ARE RECIPE CARDS?

Angel Food Recipe Cards are quick answers to immediate needs. They are snappily illustrated phrases followed by proof of scripture and often a positive prayer. When displayed on attractive easels in prominent areas of your busy home or office, they reach out and draw your thoughts back to the basics of God.

**YOUR FIRST RECIPE
WAS
MY FIRST RECIPE**

GOD HAS GOOD PLANNED FOR YOU

WITH A FUTURE AND A HOPE!

**GOD HAS GOOD PLANNED
FOR YOU
WITH A FUTURE AND A HOPE**

HOW THE RECIPE CARDS BEGAN

Since your first recipe is also my first recipe, let me share how the Recipe Cards began. I know now, that even their beginning, was not 'just by chance'.

I'm a doodler. Maybe you're one, too. You know, like when you scribble or draw designs mechanically while thinking of something else? That's how the first recipe came into existence.

In the spring of 1983, in the teacher's lounge of a large 5A high school, I sat doodling at a table. My thoughts were on a beautiful scripture the Lord had shown me the day before. Buried deep in my Bible, the Holy Spirit brought it to the surface just when I needed it. So refreshing!

> *"For I know the plans I have for you, says the Lord. They are plans for good and not for evil, to give you a future and a hope."*
> Jeremiah 29:11 (LBP)

The idea of how to clarify this scripture flashed in my mind. Quickly, I reached for a clean sheet of typing paper, folded it in half, and began sketching. Two daises and a bright shining sun appeared, with the words above saying, "God Has Good Planned for You."

"I love it!" I thought. "It's exactly what I want to say. This picture illustrates the way I feel when I hear those words."

The more I looked at the card and read the scripture, the happier I became. Having run out of plans for my life, God was showing me that He had more. He must even have them on file because His Word says He knows what they are. He also said, "The plans are for good and not for *evil*." WOW! Had I thought they might be evil? As I read on, He promised me a future and a hope.

His promise changed the whole "picture" of my life.

WHY DO I CALL THEM RECIPES?

The recipes came at a time in my life when I felt like saying, "I'm starving! I've eaten every bit of spiritual food I can find and I'm still hungry." I felt angry, bitter, negative, and disillusioned.

Then, it was as though God said, "Gwen, the food is here. I'm sorry you can't see it. I will make it simple...I will draw you a picture."

How kind of God to simplify.

Of course the pictures were drawn by my hand, but the Holy Spirit was placing them in my spirit. I even felt like He was guiding my hand, as I drew with much feeling and they turned out more accurate than if I had drawn them on my own.

As the pictures fed my hungry spirit with understanding and hope, I saw them as "recipes." Each, a set of directions preparing nourishment for my soul. As I used the recipes, accompanied by a daily portion of praise, prayer, and reading of God's Word, strength came into my life.

GOD GIVES THE RECIPES A NAME

"Angel Food" caught my attention while reading the book of *Exodus*; the part where the children of Israel struggled in their journey through the wilderness. Perhaps you too, can relate to their pains of doubt and fear as you seek survival in your personal wilderness of hopelessness, frustration, or loss of direction.

My imagination grew wild with expectancy as I watched God provide the children of Israel with manna; the food of angels.

> *"He commanded the skies to open...He opened the windows of heaven...and rained down manna for their food. He gave them bread from heaven! They ate Angels' Food!"*
> Psalms 78:23-25 (LBP)

The picture of my life changed. Suddenly, I was receiving more answers and miracles than I dreamed possible. I felt God opening the windows of heaven for *me* and pouring out so many blessings I couldn't collect them all.

> *"I will open the windows of heaven for you and pour out a blessing so great you won't have room to take it in!"*
> Malachi 3:10 (LBP)

Now, I know. It was the Holy Spirit leading me to that window. As precious crumbs of knowledge rained heavily all around me, I collected as many as possible and called them "Angel Food."

HOW DO YOU GET SOME?

The Angel Food becomes yours personally when you pick it up, taste it, and it gratifies your expectations. For example: the morsel that says, "GOD HAS GOOD PLANNED FOR YOU." Have you actually chewed it over and over in your mind? Does it taste like it's prepared especially for you? Do you find it delightful enough to share with someone else?

I hope so, because God knows the more you share; the more you benefit and the happier you become. Inevitably, the JOY OF THE LORD takes over and becomes more desirable than anything else in your life. The YEAST DOES RISE as does your circle of contacts. .

I truly believe the skies will open for you as they did for the children of Israel. God will open His windows of heaven and rain down more Angel Food than you can possibly hold. You will feel as though you will burst if you cannot share. There is absolutely no way you can keep it all to yourself.

So, share! If you have only one piece of Angel Food that you are excited about...share that! God will multiply *your blessings* when you share with others. Repetitive sharing builds confidence and strengthens belief. You are beginning a habit of sharing; not only one small piece, but many other helpful recipes God will place in your care.

GOD HELPS YOU SHARE

Each time I am fed Angel Food in the form of an answer, God sends someone in my path to share the same dish. Don't be surprised when this happens to you; just be ready!

WHAT WILL I SAY?

Since you are only a couple of steps ahead of your friend on this path out of your wilderness, look around and see who is following you. The Holy

Spirit will make use of your recent experience to guide and direct your friend. Listen to where your friend is coming from and where he wants to go. Does it sound familiar? Praise the Lord! It's easy to direct another when you have just 'been there'. You'll be so grateful when the Lord feeds you understanding, that your natural inclination will be to turn and share.

The Holy Spirit will FILL YOUR MOUTH with words of wisdom. When I recognize a friend's need, I often refer to the following recipe. Rather than trusting my own words, I choose to trust the Lord when He says:

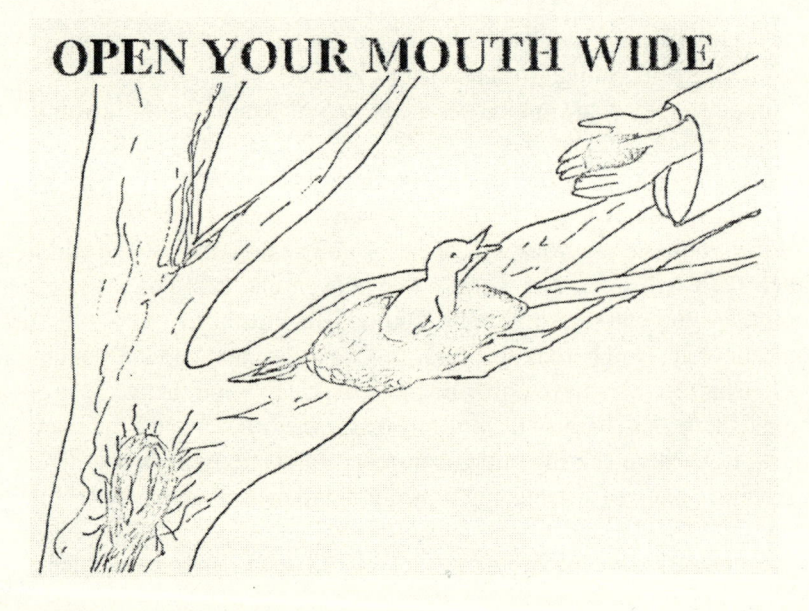

OPEN YOUR MOUTH WIDE

AND I WILL FILL IT

Once, in a position to witness, I didn't know what to say. Unsure of myself, I grasped for help. Then I remembered a part of this scripture. So testing it, I prayed, "Lord, I'm opening my mouth *wide* so that You will fill it."

He did! Naturally, I've used that prayer again and again. I even open my mouth physically, showing Him that I believe. The wisdom sent forth that day and in following situations, was definitely His knowledge. Not only did He give me the word, but He prepared the receiver to hear and understand.

"For it was I, Jehovah your God, who brought you out of the land of Egypt! Open your mouth wide and see if I won't fill it. You will receive every blessing you can use."
                    Psalms 81:10 (LBP)
"Then He touched my mouth and said, 'See, I have put My words in your mouth."
                    Jeremiah 1:9 (LBP)

And remember, the Lord says:

"I will hasten my Word to perform it."
                    Jeremiah 1:12b (KJV)

So, don't worry about what you will say when God reveals a need. Just pray, "Lord, I'm **OPENING MY MOUTH WIDE**, I know You will **FILL IT** because You said You would." And He will...He always does.

WHEN SHALL I SERVE IT ?
SERVE IT WHILE IT'S FRESH; SERVE IT WHILE IT'S HOT !

Food is much more satisfying served fresh. Spices of excitement and nutrients of extenuating blessings tend to lose their flavor with the passing of time.

As spices enhance flavor in food, so does your personal excitement enhance your experience. Your listener compares his struggle with yours. Your victory brings him hope. The Holy Spirit uses your example to clarify your friend's dilemma.

Nutrients of extenuating blessings are the multiple ways God uses to answer our original request. For example: An extenuating blessing for me was the day Charlotte Holt, a fellow teacher, came to my house for lunch. I call Charlotte my Spiritual Mother because her mature knowledge gently guides me like a loving parent.

Sharing our latest enlightenments from the Lord, I began telling Charlotte about my System of Numbers which gives me a positive outlook. This is not numerology; just something that seemed fun to me.

Capturing her interest was all the spark I needed. Spices of enthusiasm ignited as I opened *The Living Light* (a book of daily devotions) and expounded, "See the date at the top of this page? It brings my first positive hope for the day as I apply it to my NUMBER SYSTEM. Number ONE stands for God...thus POWER. TWO represents the Father and Son. THREE, as you would suspect...means the TRINITY: Father, Son, and Holy Spirit. FOUR brings the feeling of BALANCE, as does any even number. FIVE, I believe, stands for GRACE. SIX is DOUBLE TRINITY. SEVEN is God's number used throughout the Bible. TEN is DOUBLE GRACE, ELEVEN is DOUBLE POWER and so on and so on."

Charlotte shook her head and smiled, "Well, Little Chick, (she calls herself the Mother Hen) at the rate you're scratching for knowledge, you'll soon outgrow me.

I hugged her, thanking God that Christians are sincerely happy for each other.

Charlotte watched my excitement rise to its familiar crescendo. She knew I had more to say and I did.

"You know Charlotte, while thanking God for my NUMBER SYSTEM, the words from an old song came to me. They really help. Although it isn't a spiritual song, God tells us the same thing in Philippians 4:8. The song goes like this:

"Accentuate the Positive.
Eliminate the Negative.
Latch on to the Affirmative,
And don't mess with Mr. In-Between.'"

No, I didn't sing it for her. That particular gift hasn't been developed in me...yet. (Only God and I enjoy my solos.) However, encouraged by Charlotte's intrigue, I hurried to express one more thought.

"I also remain positive by using the PLUS AND MINUS SYSTEM. I interpret the PLUS as the Cross; therefore Christ and His blessings. A MINUS represents Satan and all he would like to steal from us. God is Positive...Satan is Negative."

Charlotte waited for me to finish, then commented, "That makes me think of something I heard the other day. Have you noticed how often negative thinking people use the word 'but'? The saying I heard was, THE DIFFERENCE BETWEEN A LAMB AND A GOAT IS THE BUT."

THE DIFFERENCE BETWEEN A LAMB AND A GOAT

IS THE "BUT"

I could be free "but" life's too hard.

We both laughed. It's funny and yet it isn't. How often we've heard comments like, "I could have climbed that mountain...BUT...I guess I gave up too soon." Or, they begin a positive statement such as, "Susan is a very kind person...BUT...have you seen the awful way she keeps house?" The MINUS in this statement promptly cancelled the PLUS.

So, the "number system" led to a correlation of "plusses and minuses" which included an old song. I saw each as an extenuating blessing to improve my positive thinking. Charlotte added the fourth when she described the difference between a lamb and a goat. The following day revealed a fifth blessing in this chain of events.

Bobbie, a divorcee with a young son, came to see me. Her life clouded with disappointments, she is trying to use positive terms. Each time she tells something good that's happening to her, her face glows with appreciation for God's blessings. Then, however, here comes the "but."

Today, Bobbie's conversation followed the usual pattern. I soon heard the "but." This time I had a tangible answer.

Smiling with understanding, I handed her a picture (Recipe Card) of

Charlotte's fourth blessing, and said, "Bobbie, I have something for you."

Excitable laughter crossed her face as she looked at the drawing and said, "You'll never believe this! My mother says that about me...that I always end a sentence with a 'but'. I'm taking this recipe home and putting it on the easel in my kitchen. I want to see it and practice it."

Bobbie, rushing in to visit so close behind Charlotte, allowed spices of excitement to remain vibrant with flavor. I easily remembered *all* the ideas I wanted to share. God's timing is perfect.

So, dear friend, when the Lord sends you a beautiful piece of Angel Food...know that another hungry soul will come seeking. Be prepared to serve...and please,

SERVE IT WHILE IT'S HOT!

SERVE IT

WHILE IT'S FRESH!

SERVE IT WHILE IT'S FRESH!

IF NOT A WHOLE MEAL...PERHAPS A SNACK

In the working world of today, our path through the wilderness has more the appearance of a busy freeway. When the hungry don't have time for a full course...offer a snack. Pull an appropriate recipe card and say, "Here, you look like you need this."

**IF NOT A MEAL
PERHAPS
A SNACK!**

After examining it, they'll likely respond to you as they have to me. "You're right. That's exactly what I need," and be on their hurried way.

For many, this snack awakens dormant taste buds, enticing them back for more. Some days I simply slip one in a teacher's mailbox or leave it on his or her desk. The Holy Spirit knows when the time is right.

However, the more you practice listening to the Holy Spirit and become familiar with the way He works, the more accurate becomes your diagnosis of individual hunger "pangs." Since you are willing to share, the Holy Spirit promises to guide you. Remember, He is sending people in your path. You are not necessarily seeking them. Try to remain prepared for those He sends.

No, these recipes are not fliers or circulars used in mass distribution. They are used with all respect to the Word of God, as you sense His Spirit leading you.

HIS WORD WILL NOT RETURN VOID. It will accomplish all He sends it to do. Secure in your heart that God is sending the Word...you know HE WILL HASTEN TO PERFORM IT. Isn't that a relief; knowing you are not responsible for making His Word come true? You simply deliver the message; God does the work.

A TYPICAL SNACK

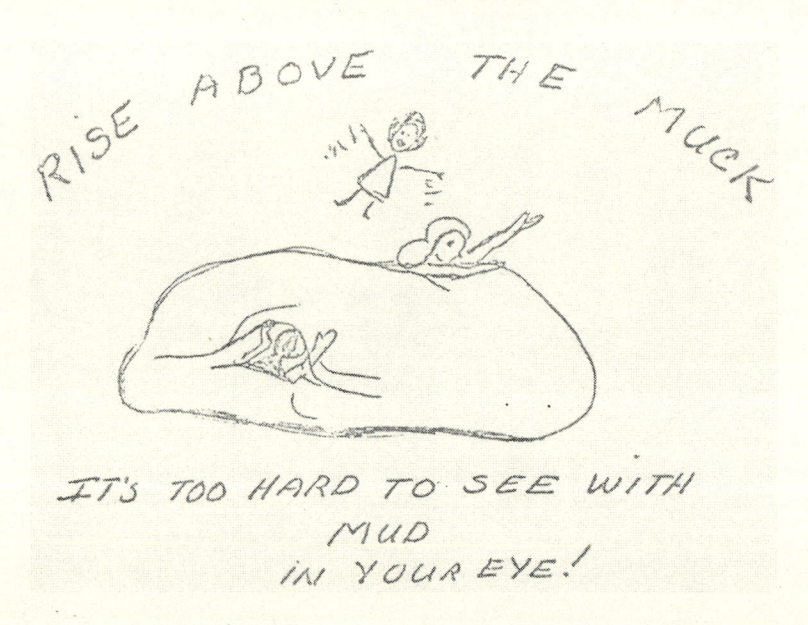

RISE ABOVE THE MUCK

IT'S TOO HARD TO SEE WITH MUD IN YOUR EYE!

This card consistently brings a chuckle and helps the receiver view his plight from a different angle. It makes him aware that everyday problems can pull him down.

The little girl flapping her arms at the top of the picture acts as an incentive for us to do the same, i.e. rise above.

To uplift, encourage, and pass the news that GOD HAS GOOD PLANNED FOR YOU is your purpose in sharing these recipes. Although your friend delightfully accepts this card as a reminder to RISE ABOVE TRIVIA: the warmth of your concern presents a stronger message.

So a SNACK served with LOVE may be just the ENERGY BOOST your friend needs to steer gracefully and confidently: cruising through the approaching traffic of his or her busy day.

Now, aren't you glad you had a SNACK handy? As you watch your friend driving away, I see you already turning your head looking for someone else to share with. "Ain't" this fun? Who said Christians don't have fun? Are you praising God? Are you thanking Him for including you in His plan? Are you already asking Him to use you again? I bet you are...and He will!

BACK TO THE TABLE
FOR
GOD'S GIFT OF LOVE

Well, dear friend, you appear quite comfortable now. The way you're eyeing the food I can tell you're anxious to try some. I'm so glad.

You've read how the recipes came about and how to use them. Are you ready for this one?

It's the dish of God's Love. I tasted it many times in my life...but never prepared like this.

Praise the Lord! This is the way God meant it to be prepared and served. This time, as I ate, finally digesting the truth;

IT FREED ME...TO BE ME.
GOD LOVES YOU WITH AN UNCONDITIONAL LOVE
NO STRINGS ATTACHED
JUST BECAUSE YOU'RE YOU.

NO STRINGS ATTACHED

I'M FREE!

God loves you *just because you are His.* He loves you with an unconditional love. He doesn't say you must be perfect before receiving His love...He loves you just as you are today, right this minute. There's no need to *prove* your worth to Him...He knows!

Praise the Lord! You don't have to prove yourself to anyone anymore. Not to parents, spouse, children, or others...and *especially* not to yourself. Your best recommendation is that God loves you the way He made you. You are good enough for Him...you are good enough for yourself. Not only good enough, but very special. Remember:

O REMEMBER O
YOU'RE A KING'S KID

SO SMILE

How's LOVE tasting? Pretty Sweet? I'm glad! But hold on, it becomes sweeter yet...when you stop reading about it and actually put it to use.

Do this by making a conscious effort to find various 'forms of love' in everything you do; from the time you throw off your covers in the morning and jump out of bed, until you peacefully snuggle under them again at night. Purposely dissect everything you see and do; looking for sparks of love. Notice your mind becoming more alert to it's environment, as it becomes saturated by discovering love...in a child making mud pies, a flower appearing to raise its face thanking God for the morning dew, a tired husband graciously repairing your vacuum cleaner, or in yourself washing dishes to the glory of God.

Once you understand the enormous span of opportunities available for demonstrating love, you become avid in your desires to assert your own method of loving. Good! Go ahead! Love! PRACTICE! PRACTICE! PRACTICE! Love in as many ways as you know how. Creating this beautiful habit, you'll soon find yourself surrounded by countless blessings.

Success of this dish is guaranteed when you practice loving others the way God loves you...with NO STRINGS ATTACHED.

Watch out for strings: you've attached to yourself; you've attached to others; or you've allowed Satan to attach to you.

```
          SNIP THEM QUICK
             BE FREE
              FLY!
```

Remember, you're no puppet. You have 'freedom of choice'. I pray you choose to release these strings and receive your freedom in the joy of the Lord.

Should you like a specific recipe, I found this one in God's Big Cook Book and labeled it:

RULES OF THE HOUSE
Let Love Be Our Greatest Aim. I Cor. 14:1

BE PATIENT AND KIND
NEVER JEALOUS OR ENVIOUS
NEVER BOASTFUL OR PROUD
NEVER HAUGHTY OR SELFISH OR RUDE
NOT DEMAND MY OWN WAY
NOT BE IRRITABLE OR TOUCHY
NOR HOLD GRUDGES
TRY NOT TO NOTICE
WHEN OTHERS DO ME WRONG
NEVER BE GLAD ABOUT INJUSTICE
RATHER, REJOICE WHEN TRUTH WINS OUT
LOYAL TO MY FRIENDS - NO MATTER
WHAT THE COST
ALWAYS BELIEVE IN THEM
EXPECT THE BEST OF THEM
STAND MY GROUND IN
DEFENDING THEM

I Corinthians 13:4-7 (LBP)

MANNA
THE BREAD OF LIFE

"The hors d'oeuvres were great," you say. "And God's Dish of Love, was even better. They certainly served the purpose of whetting my appetite for something stronger, like bread or meat. Will you be serving that soon?"

Absolutely! As a matter of fact, that's exactly the dish I'm placing before you now. I'm sure it looks familiar. It should. It's Manna: the true bread from Heaven. In John 6:33-35, God refers to it as the "Bread of Life" which is necessary for salvation. The following scripture is your bread:

For God so loved the world, that He gave His only begotten Son, that whosoever believeth in Him should not perish, but have everlasting life. For God sent not His son into the world to condemn the world; but that the world through Him might be saved.
John 3:16-17 (KJV)

I'm assuming you've already tasted this food. But, can we ever receive too much of God's food...His promise of our salvation? Can we ever thank Him enough for sending His precious Son to die for us: taking all our sins upon Himself? No, we can't. No life or meal is complete without the bread of John 3:16

"If..."the extent of your starvation is more than you or I realize and you haven't tasted the Dish of Salvation, which is the 'Bread of Life', please do so now.

Don't be afraid to talk to God. He is waiting to hear from you. He wants you to come to Him. The Bible says:

*Yet the Lord still waits for you to come
to Him, so He can show you His love.*
Isaiah 30:18 (LBP)

Salvation is very personal...just between you and God. It may occur in church or in the privacy of your home. Although it's encouraging to have a Christian friend with you at the time, it is not essential.

When you decide you really do love the Lord and you don't want to spend one more day without Him...tell Him!

Using your own words, tell God that you know you are a sinner (we all were) and that you are asking Him to forgive you. The minute you ask, you are forgiven. Tell Him that you do believe in Jesus Christ, His Son who died for you and was raised from the dead.

As you are telling God that you are giving your heart, life, and desires to Him...you'll feel a joy and release. You'll realize that you are no longer alone.

Thank God for saving you because that is just what happened. Praise Him over and over because before this moment, you were alone and condemned. Now you have a Father, Savior, Brother, and Friend. You'll never be alone again and you'll never again be unloved.

Now that Jesus has come into your life, you'll want to take the next step. In fact, I doubt that anyone can prevent you from taking it. When something this wonderful happens to you, it's almost impossible to keep it to yourself. You feel you must tell someone.

If you're not sure what the next step is, don't worry. God directs you through His Word as He asks you to make your profession in His Son an open one for others to see. For those who are new in Christ, the church is an excellent place to begin...as it was for me.

AS A LITTLE CHILD

At nine years of age I sat on the front pew in a small frame church in Bandera, Texas, listening to my daddy preach. Hearing him tell about the love of Jesus, my young eyes filled with tears and I wanted more than anything to belong to Jesus...to receive that love...and someday to live with Him in Heaven.

During the alter call at the end of the service I was puzzled. Only adults walked forward and gave their hearts to Jesus. I wondered if I was too young.

Feeling obligated to remain in my seat, it seemed church would never be over. When it was, I thought Daddy would never stop shaking hands and talking to people. I wished he would hurry. I had something important to ask him.

Daddy finally waved goodbye to the last family leaving the parking lot. Taking my hand, we walked across the open area between the church and the parsonage. He was watching my face. He probably knew what I was thinking. But, I couldn't ask him yet. I had to find...just the right words.

Opening the wire gate and entering our yard, we passed the abundant blue Morning Glories Daddy and I had planted. Queen, our border collie, rousing from her nap on the front porch, ran down the wooden steps to greet us. Jumping and leaping and turning circles, she received our pats of affection and followed us back up the steps to the screen door.

As we entered the house, Daddy took off his coat and tie and sat down to rest in his rocking chair. I ran on through the dining room to see what Mother was cooking in the kitchen.

Mashed potatoes, brown gravy, and fried chicken...Great! But, pleasing me more, was seeing her busy and the probability of her remaining so for awhile.

"Good!" I thought. "I can have time with Daddy alone." The question taking form now, I knew what I wanted to ask.

I ran to Daddy and hugged his neck then sat on the floor in front of him. With my knees bent under, and sitting back on my heels, I said, "Daddy, can't little kids come to Jesus?"

He laughed, and with a twinkle in his eye, (or was that possibly a tear of joy?) he put his arms around me and said, "Oh yes, my daughter, little children most certainly can come to Jesus. Don't you remember the Bible verse where Jesus said, 'Suffer the little children to come unto me, and forbid them not: for of such is the kingdom of God.'?"

"Does that mean I can be saved?"

"Yes it does," my Daddy said, and right then and there, we kneeled and I asked Jesus to come into my life. Praise the Lord for Christian daddies.

Jesus does love little children....just as He loves the child in each of us, regardless of our age. After Jesus said to let the children come to Him, Mark 10:16 tells us He took them up in His arms, put His hands upon them, and blessed them. Isn't that beautiful?

That night at church, I could hardly wait for the invitation. As the first note sounded from the piano, before the congregation could rise, I was out of my seat and racing down the aisle...to tell the world:

"I am a Christian!"

Not haltingly, not ashamed, not embarrassed...but saying the words boldly with pride. Not questioning my worthiness; simply loving Jesus and cherishing His love for me.

My first thoughts, following my salvation experience, were of my friends. So with the urgency of childhood, I ran, seeking them. They must learn they too could become Christians. And, using the simplest terms, I told them how.

"All we have to do is say we're sorry for our sins, and tell Jesus we want to be His child. My daddy says we're not too young."

As soon as this good news spread, many children did profess their faith in Christ (including my younger brother Bruce) and were baptized by my father in the Medina River.

Many times in the bible, God uses the example of a child to show the kind of faith He wants us to have in Him. Just as a young child believes everything his father tells him, God wants us to believe everything He tells us. Even if we are ninety years old when we accept the Lord. We are still His child. His desire is for us to "come trusting..." leaving behind our worries, cares, and sophisticated philosophies as we make Him Lord of our life.

It is through belief in Christ Jesus that we claim His promise of life after death and more abundant life on earth. Although our faith may not seem as strong as we would like at the beginning...Praise the Lord, we are no longer alone. He is here to help. He delights in watching His children grow. And, when we believe what He tells us, growth is much easier.

God knows we are not born 'full-grown', neither do we come into His Kingdom that way. He loves us as 'new-born babies.' That is a very special time for Him. But it is not His intention that we remain babies. *Many* gifts, pleasures, and abilities await us through maturation.

BABY FOOD IS GREAT FOR BABIES
BUT
OH THE JOY OF SITTING AT THE TABLE WITH THE GROWN-UPS!

> *And I, brethren, could not speak unto you as*
> *unto spiritual, but as unto carnal, even as*
> *unto babes in Christ.*
> *I have fed you with milk, and not with meat:*
> *for hitherto ye were not able to bear it....*
> I Corinthians 3:1-2 (KJV)

Baby Christians are those who accept the Lord as their Savior; making a public profession of faith, and in many instances receive Baptism. Jesus claims them as His because they have accepted Him. Yes, they are saved...but somewhere, somehow they stop growing. Often, the reason is their environment.

If your parents are suffering from malnutrition, it's likely that you are too. Even if your parents are Christians, they may have gone so long without eating spiritual food that they no longer realize their need. Neither do they realize your need. They don't know you are hungry.

But, Praise the Lord, *you* know you are hungry and *you* know you want to grow. Do you remember the growing pains we had as kids? Our legs ached. Some of us had that awful acne, and our bodies went through the frustrating changes of puberty. Then, WOW! It happened! The day finally came when we felt all grown up...no more dolls and toy trucks. We knew our growing pains had been worth it when we found ourselves sitting at the table with the grownups and eating grownup food.

Now that you know there is more to Christianity than Baby Food, you'll seek until you find it. You won't be satisfied without that special food that makes you strong enough to become what God has planned for you.

The best advice I can give is to KEEP ON LOOKING. God promises that you will find it if you don't give up.

The example in the eleventh chapter of Luke presents a clear picture of persistent prayer. The story is about a man who, having gone to bed for the night, doesn't want to get up and answer the door when his neighbor continues knocking and asking for bread.

> *"But I'll tell you this...though he won't do it*
> *as a friend, if you keep knocking long enough*
> *he will get up and give you everything you want*
> *...just because of your persistence.*
> *And so it is with prayer...keep on asking and*

*you will keep on getting; keep on looking and
you will keep on finding; knock and the door
will be opened.
Everyone who asks, receives; all who seek, find;
and the door is opened to everyone who knocks."*
Luke 11:8-10 (LBP)

That's how it happened to me. I asked, and sought, and knocked ...many times. Perhaps I wasn't hungry enough earlier to keep on seeking. But, when I became very, very hungry and sought with all my heart (Deuteronomy 4:29), the Lord was true to His Word and fed me. My missing dish was: THE HOLY SPIRIT.

Don't Be Afraid To Knock!

MY MISSING DISH

The Holy Spirit! I feel like shouting at the mention of His name. As I taste true knowledge, direction, and freedom, I can't thank God enough for the addition of the Holy Spirit to my daily diet.

The Holy Spirit represents the TRUE MEAT as the main course of the feast the Lord has me serving you today. If you're familiar with this dish I'm sure it's one of your favorites and you're glad it's on the menu.

Go ahead and eat. If you don't mind, I'll join you as just thinking about this dish makes my mouth water.

When seeking the Holy Spirit I read many books about Him, but what I really wanted to hear was...how it happened to someone else. Unfamiliar with the Holy Spirit, I didn't know what to expect. Since my experience however, I've learned that there is more than one way to receive the Baptism of the Holy Spirit. I like the simple way God chose for me; it makes it easier to share with His other Baby Christians. They need this experience. It's imperative for above average growth. So, from one friend to another:

**THIS IS HOW GOD FED ME
THE DISH OF THE HOLY SPIRIT**

"God has deliberately chosen to use ideas the world considers foolish and of little worth in order to shame those people considered by the world as wise and great."
I Corinthians 1:17 (LBP)

In a small room in Kingwood High School, three to five teachers prayed daily for students, teachers, administrators, and personal needs. Since prayer was not allowed in schools, we referred to the room as the 'catacombs'.

I wasn't in the group long before I realized these women had something I didn't. My prayers usually consisted of moaning and groaning, complaining and crying. My life seemed useless. I felt weak and helpless where I wanted to be strong. I hated cowards. I hated my crying, and I hated the word 'impossible.' Yet, I was acting out each of these parts.

These women never cried when they prayed. They acted as though they believed God would answer their prayers...even so far as healing people.

Can you believe they told me not to pray "God's will be done" concerning healing? They said it *is* God's will for people to be well. I couldn't understand how I could possibly pray any other way. However, the way I prayed for "God's will," did seem like some kind of 'security blanket', just in case I had too little faith to pull off a miracle. You see, I thought it was *my faith* that worked miracles. Now, I know it is *God* who works miracles.

These women were a new breed of Christians to me. But the most exciting, was a beautiful red head named Joan (pronounced Jo Ann) Strong. In charge of Visual Aids in the school library, Joan supervised our ever growing Fellowship of Christian Athletes. Although she has a figure like Sophia Loren and I'm intrigued by her lovely clothes, there is absolutely nothing that compares to the brightness of her smile.

Joan became my enticement to the Holy Spirit. I had never met anyone who was that consistently happy. When there were problems, she always seemed to have an answer. The phrase I feel most typifies her is, "The joy of the Lord is my strength." Her personality so radiant; she actually appeared to glow.

When near her, I somehow felt closer to whatever I was looking for. Turning to God, I said, "Lord, I want that! I want what Joan has."

When I found out what Joan had was the Holy Spirit, I said, "Okay Lord, Joan's life shows me that there obviously is *more*. You said, 'Ask and ye shall receive'...well, I'm asking. I want more. I want to be filled with the Holy Spirit."

Although a Christian the majority of my life, now in my forties, I felt like a child among adults. There was so much to learn.

First of all, how does an ole Southern Baptist go about getting filled with the Holy Spirit? The only answer I could come up with was to seek and ask questions.

Taking the only information I found about Spirit Filled Christians, I began asking about the 'tongues'. Not everyone who is filled with the Holy Spirit speaks in tongues, but in my limited knowledge, I decided this must be the place to start.

I was later to find out that there are two types of tongues. One is 'the gift of tongues' for the body of believers. This is spoken out in a church service and must have an interpretation by the one who gives the message in tongues or by another Spirit filled Christian. Not everyone has this. But I am telling you about the kind of tongues that is available to any Christian who has received the Baptism in the Holy Spirit.

So again I prayed, "Lord, if there's more, I want it. I want all You have to offer me." I bought every book I could find on the Holy Spirit. Books I had read earlier, out of curiosity, denying my need for the Holy Spirit, no longer seemed like the same books. Now that I believed, they were full of life and sustaining knowledge.

A friend told me that all I had to do was ask the Holy Spirit to come into my life and that He would. So, I asked Him, and He did. But how could I know this for sure? I felt I needed a sign. That's when I asked the Lord to let me speak in tongues. The Bible says this is a sign that a Christian has been baptized in the Holy Spirit.

Reading that the physical way to receive your 'spiritual or prayer language' as 'tongues' is sometimes called, is to relax your tongue, jaws, and the muscles of your mouth, I proceeded to attempt this. I was to give my tongue over to the Lord and he would give me words I didn't understand in my natural language.

This didn't make sense to me until I found out how much control the tongue has over the body. Boy, does it ever. If any one part of the body needs to be given over to the Lord, it is certainly the tongue.

> *"So also the tongue is a small thing, but what enormous damage it can do. A great forest can be set on fire by one tiny spark. And the tongue is a flame of fire. It is full of wickedness, and poisons every part of the body. And the tongue is set on fire by hell itself, and can turn our whole lives into a blazing flame of destruction and disaster."*
> James 4:5,6 (LBP)

Although I tried and tried, nothing happened. A void remained in my throat and no words came out.

Then, one day while putting on my make-up at the dressing table in our bathroom, I tried again. I relaxed my mouth, wiggled my tongue around, and told God I was giving my mouth to Him. I began thinking of ways to praise Him. I even lifted my hands and arms toward Heaven; a form of worship I refused to accept while visiting one of those 'different' kind of churches. However, now it seemed the only way to show Him I was truly offering my all.

Relaxed and releasing myself to God, I experienced a feeling of elation. Words did come from my mouth. Strange little words...sounding like baby gibberish.

Thinking now about the women I had curiously watched at church praying in tongues, I hadn't believed them. They sounded unreal to me. I had to laugh at myself. If anyone heard this, they certainly wouldn't believe me either.

> *"Even so, if an unsaved person, or someone who doesn't have these gifts, comes to church and hears you all talking in other languages, he is likely to think you are crazy."*
> I Corinthians 14:23 (LBP)

Well, this baby talk did sound silly, but the feeling of release wasn't silly, nor did it feel silly. It felt great! After all, what is so unusual about someone sounding strange as they begin a new language? We've all laughed with babies as they tried their first word...yet, we recognized the word. I even recall the way my first grade class of Mexican American students laughed when I tried to speak Spanish. Although they recognized the words, my unfamiliarity with their language made them laugh. I laughed too, but was excited about the possibilities of a better communication...as is our prayer language.

Ecstasy over my new prayer language made me feel like Liza Doolittle in the Broadway show of *My Fair Lady*. I kept saying, "I've got it, I've got it, by George, I think I've got it." I wrote down the first three words the way they sounded to me..."Que Anni Luna." I think they mean "Jesus loves me."

I could hardly wait to tell the ladies in the prayer group I thought I had received my prayer language. You see, the human side of me still needed confirmation. But, Praise the Lord, God understands that side of us too and He is able to provide all our needs.

On the way to school Monday morning; alone in our family van, I began singing. Then I began singing in my new language. Filled with happiness, praising God in my heart, I allowed my mouth to make any sound it desired. I was high! I mean to tell you I was high! This experience was better than I had dared dream it could be. I was free! Although the doubt was quickly fading in the presence of such evidence, I still wondered, "Is this it, Lord? Do I truly have my prayer language?"

My thoughts turned momentarily to the way my friends had smiled knowingly when I told them I wanted the Baptism of the Holy Spirit and the gift of tongues. They hadn't offered to tell me how; they just said that since I wanted it, I would receive it. Each day as I told them that I hadn't received it yet, they would confidently say, "You will." It's evident to me now that they saw the intensity of my desire and were also familiar with the verse:

> *"And ye shall seek me and find me, when ye shall search for me with all your heart."*
> Jeremiah 29:13 (KJV)

God knew I wasn't mature enough to recognize His confirmations about the work of the Holy Spirit, so guess who He placed in my path? You're right...Joan Strong.

As I turned the van into the school parking lot, Joan was getting out of her small car. I ran to her with a silly grin on my face. I had to ask her, "Joan, can you speak your prayer language anytime you want to?"

She smiled and said, "Yes."

Then I inquired, "Would you speak it for me now? I've never heard someone I know personally, speak that way. I want to know what it really sounds like."

In her gracious, understanding way, she began to speak. I can't write it down, but it was beautiful.

Hope rose in my heart. Although Joan's prayer carried all the fluidness of a familiar language, and mine had the stuttering staccato of a beginner, I sensed their similarity.

Hesitant to continue, yet not able to stop myself, I began telling her what I thought I had received. "But, mine sounds like I'm from Africa or sometimes it sounds a little Hawaiian."

After I told her the first three words and asked if she thought I 'had it,' do you know what she said?

"Yes, Gwen, that's it," she said. "You have your prayer language."

Hugging her right there in the middle of the parking lot, I felt like dancing and shouting because I knew, I knew, I knew...that the Holy Spirit had entered my life. Oh, how I praised God for sending this beautiful red-haired angel to confirm my prayer language.

How often we thank someone for a gift without realizing its true value. Not until we use it over and over again, can we appreciate its worth.

Now I consistently pray in my prayer language as well as in English. I don't compare it to other people's languages and I don't use it for show; it's just between the Holy Spirit and me. It doesn't matter to Him what it sounds like in the natural. He recognizes it and knows what I mean. It's not the talk anyway; it's the release. The release of my will for something better...God's will.

Some say our prayer language is a means of communication Satan cannot intercept or understand. I felt this to be true as more power came into my life even before I found the following scripture.

> *"But ye shall receive power, after that the*
> *Holy Ghost is come upon you."*
> Acts 1:8 (KJV)

The word best describing the way I feel as I pray in tongues, is "infinity." God is infinite and as I attempt to praise Him, my longings channel upward as through an endless tunnel. Human words are insufficient to tell God how much I love Him.

Then, as I hurt sometimes and am not sure why I hurt, I try to tell God about my pain. Again, I can't find the right words. However, as I release my cares through my prayer language, the Holy Spirit reveals my source of pain, and God returns an answer in a language I can understand.

Thus, He directed me to another scripture:

> *"The Holy Spirit helps us with our daily problems and in our*
> *praying. For we don't even know what we should pray for,*
> *nor how to pray as we should; but the Holy Spirit prays for us*
> *with such feeling that it cannot be expressed in words. And the*
> *Father who knows all hearts knows, of course, what the Spirit*

is saying as He pleads for us in harmony with God's own will."
Romans 8:26-27 (LBP)

Praise God! Jesus did not leave us defenseless when He went to Heaven. Rather, He sent the Holy Spirit to guide, direct, and comfort us. Read about the Comforter in chapter two of the book of Acts and I Corinthians, chapter fourteen.

Spirit-filled Christians also speak another language quite different from what many are use to hearing. It's a positive language of hope and gratitude. There is a zesty expectancy in the way they seem to know GOD HAS SOMETHING GOOD PLANNED FOR THEM. Should a suspicious onlooker be around for any amount of time, he will see something good happen to these Christians. When it does, their joy overflows as they become as excited about small everyday miracles as they do the big ones.

HOW CAN ONE HEAR THE HOLY SPIRIT ?

Are you wondering how one hears the Holy Spirit? I did too. Again, no one actually told me and I didn't remember reading it in a book.

In fact, I didn't know where to look. So, I went straight to the Head Man and this is what He taught me.

The first step is to ask.

The second step is to listen with all your heart and expect to hear.

Begin looking for clues. Such as a Bible verse speaking personally to you. Notice environmental clues associated with the will of God.

When you think you hear the Holy Spirit speaking to you: obey! In these beginning training sessions the Lord will allow you to see a very obvious result. This will confirm that you did hear the Holy Spirit.

Once you hear and obey, continue to practice. If you stop listening; He'll stop talking.

Once you've followed the directions of the Holy Spirit, you will no longer be satisfied by your previously limited life style.

To ASK, LISTEN, EXPECT, LOOK FOR CLUES, OBEY, and PRACTICE...makes sense to the practical thinker. However, how I learned these basic truths may call on your spiritual tolerance.

The following experiences may seem strange. But then, we are each created so very different. God must teach us where we are, as we are.

THE HOLY SPIRIT IS A GENTLEMAN

The Holy Spirit is a gentleman. He doesn't force His friendship. If you want to know Him, *you* must invite him into your life.

Once He enters, He speaks ever so quietly.

I found this to be true the day I got busy and forgot I had asked to hear Him. He didn't forget. The gentleman that He is, He found a way to show me.

Arranging a new office in my home, I decided the beige touch tone phone in the kitchen would look better than the present black one. I proceeded to make the change.

As I reached to disconnect the black phone, something seemed to tell me "No." I couldn't think of any reason not to, so I tried again.

Three times I reached to remove the phone from its connection. Each time I heard the word, "no." It wasn't a strong "No...." Just loud enough to make me wonder if I had heard it.

Searching for an answer, I remembered my morning prayer to hear the Holy Spirit.

But surely that wasn't the Holy Spirit talking to me. No...He would recognize the importance of color coordination in my new office.

"This is ridiculous," I thought. So, stubbornly ignoring that Inner Voice and wanting my own way, I unplugged the phones and made the exchange.

"Now, that looks better," I nearly convinced myself.

"I like the touch tone. It makes me feel important," my mind continued to argue. "Besides, my business is growing so fast I have a lot of dialing to do. Yes, this will definitely be faster."

Efficiently set up for business, I wondered who I should call first. Checking my list of customers, I picked the one most likely to be out of product and proceeded to dial.

Surprise! As I pressed the keys, they no longer made their impressive musical sounds. I couldn't get a connection. The crazy thing wouldn't work!

Embarrassed, I quickly ran from my office to the kitchen and from the kitchen to my office replacing the phones...wishing the Holy Spirit couldn't see me. Let's face it! I made a foolish decision when I chose 'not to listen' to the Holy Spirit.

I felt like saying, "Oh, so that was You. Okay, I got the message. You know more than I do. I didn't know the beige phone wouldn't work in this room, but You did. It wasn't that You didn't want me to have the fancy equipment; You just wanted me to have the best. You wanted me to have something that would work."

"Thanks for caring for me," I began to pray with joyful awareness. "From now on, I'm listening to You because You have *all* the answers. You know I like action; I like to see things work fast...and I don't have time for anymore of my 'goof-ups'. I'm sorry I didn't recognize You."

It was as though He said, "It's alright, Gwen. You did get the message. Now that you recognize My voice, there are many ways I can help you."

Hardly a day passes now that I don't tell Him, "Thanks, Holy Spirit, I know you DIRECT MY PATH AND MAKE IT SURE."

Let Proverbs 3:5-6 encourage you also.

> *"Trust in the Lord with all thine heart; and lean not unto thine own understanding. In all thy ways acknowledge Him and He shall direct thy paths."*

CLUES

The same day I learned another form of communication with the Holy Spirit.

While still praising God for showing me how the Holy Spirit can reach us through a gentle nudge, I picked up a small card lying on a box in my new office. It was from a set of scripture cards Mother kept on the breakfast table when I was a child. "How unusual," I thought, "that one should show up today." I hadn't remembered seeing them for years.

It read, "...weeping may endure for a night, but JOY COMETH IN THE MORNING." (Psalms 30:5).

My spirit leaped within me. Dare I hope this was another message from the Holy Spirit? Would He choose to reinforce my belief so soon?

My mind raced ahead and locked in on the only thing "Joy in the morning" could mean. My Cambridge order was coming in.

All those customers I tried to pacify on the phone could now continue their blessed weight loss.

The next morning, with the scripture card beside my typewriter, I turned to look out my office window.

What I saw, took my breath away. It was the most beautiful UPS delivery truck I had ever seen. It was my Cambridge order!

I flew out of my office, down the hall, and was racing through the kitchen to beat my son and husband to the door.

When I threw the door open, the poor delivery man was aghast at what he saw. Stumbling backward, he reached for the security of a possible escape.

Jumping up and down in the middle of her kitchen, was an apparently 'crazy woman' laughing, waving her arms, and shouting, "JOY IN THE MORNING...OH, JOY IN THE MORNING..."

The frightened man quickly slid the boxes through the door. Then, fled past my husband and teenage son who were rolling in hysterics on the front porch.

"Confirmation Plus..".I called it. I thought, but didn't know for sure that I was hearing from the Holy Spirit again, until I saw the truck.

"What a wild and wooly scene you created.," you must be thinking. It was! I couldn't contain the joy. Had I found a million dollars, I doubt I could have felt more exhilaration.

Through a clue, the Holy Spirit had communicated to me the encouragement of a coming event.

Will you act like that when the Holy Spirit speaks to you? Not always. But sometimes!

You will want to experience this same type of joy as often as you can. It doesn't come every day, but when it does, you'll love it.

And remember the Holy Spirit is a gentleman. With His power to control your environment, the ony people present will be those who love you. Or someone like my delivery man who must have changed his route. It was my first and last time to see the man.

EVERYDAY EVENTS

Knowing now that the Holy Spirit speaks quietly and through clues, I decided to find out what would happen should I spend the whole day, trying to hear Him.

So, the next morning, seated at my kitchen table, having read my Bible, I prayed..."Okay, Lord, now I'm ready to listen. Really listen...all day long."

I relaxed and waited. Soon, I felt a familiar nudging. The Holy Spirit was talking to me. Yes, I felt sure it was Him. But surely I misunderstod His message. It certainly didn't sound spiritual.

PUT HOT SOAPY WATER IN THE SINK

"Put hot soapy water in the sink," He repeated.

Deciding I had argued enough, I said, "Okay, I'll PUT HOT SOAPY WATER IN THE SINK."

Before I knew it, the kitchen was sparkling and so was I. What woman can resist a sink full of warm soapy bubbles? I couldn't. How clever of the Holy Spirit. He knows the inspiration of a clean kitchen.

In 2 Kings 20:1, God says, "Set thine house in order...."

Cleaning my kitchen was the very thing I needed that morning. It was the boost that got me busy about my work.

Accepting the Holy Spirit's voice, I claimed the following scripture.

> *"In all thy ways acknowledge Him, and He shall direct they paths."*
> Proverbs 3:6 (KJV)

Thrilled by the results of following what seemed a strange command, I said, "Well, Holy Spirit, that was simple. What do we do now?"

"Go roll your hair and fix your face," He seemed to say. "You can listen to Barbara Arbo's tapes on prayer at the same time."

How silly this all seemed. I began to giggle. What if my friends saw me and heard me saying this was from God? Then I began to laugh out loud. No matter what others thought, I was having fun. So was the Holy Spirit. Not only is He clever, but He must have a great sense of humor.

Marching straight to my dressing table, I followed His second direction. Then, joking with the Holy Spirit as I removed the hot curlers from my hair, I said, "Now, I guess You're going to tell me what to wear today? Naturally, it will save me time and be the perfect choice."

You guessed it. He directed me straight to my blue pants suit in the closet. There was no doubt in my mind. I knew immediately it was the one.

Sooner than usual, I was dressed with my hair looking great. With the Holy Spirit as my beautician, how could I look less?

Just in time too, because at that moment, the door bell rang. It was my customer, the professional model who always looks perfect. Even today, returning from her ballet class without a sign of perspiration nor a wrinkle in her leotards.

How embarrassing if she had found my kitchen in a mess and me in my ragged house coat. "Thanks Holy Spirit for your loving prompting that made me feel equal."

This procedure continued through the rest of that day, on into the next, and remains with me today. When one finds a 'game plan' this good, it would be showing a lack of wisdom to change it.

The Holy Spirit encourages me with this verse:

> *"I advise you to obey only the Holy Spirit's instructions.*
> *He will tell you where to go and what to do, and then*
> *you won't always be doing the wrong things...."*
>   Galatians 5:16 (LBP)

However, the verse I repeatedly used during this practice session was:

> *"And if you leave God's paths and go astray,*
> *you will hear a Voice behind you say, 'No,*
> *this is the way; walk here.'"*
>   Isaiah 30:21 (LBP)

I'M GLAD I LISTENED

I learned three lessons that day. One, that God may ask you to do something that seems silly.

If you think I was silly, read Ezekiel four and five and see all the things God told Ezekiel to do. If I had been there before I learned to hear the Holy Spirit, I would have been the first to laugh. I would definitely have written him off as insane. But God always has a reason for asking us to do something. From now on, I don't care how crazy it "seems," I plan to do it.

The second lesson was OBEDIENCE. Obedience in small tasks prepares us for obedience in the larger ones.

Third, I found what FUN it is having the Holy Spirit as our best friend.

So if you haven't tried the dish of "Hearing the Holy Spirit" perhaps now is the time. Psalms 34:8 says, "O *taste* and see that the Lord is good...."

Well, my honored guest, I have served you the dish of the Holy Spirit in the simplest recipe I own...the way God served me. I want to serve it fresh, before the spices of growth cover its simplicity.

Many chefs far exceed me in explaining the Holy Spirit. Buy their books and read as much as you hunger for. God will direct you to the books that fill your need.

The greatest Chef is God. The greatest Cook Book ever published is His Bible. If you don't have one with an index or concordance; get it. *The Living Bible Paraphrased* has greatly enlightened God's Word for me. Yet, I return to the *King James Version* for comparison and memory work.

Yes, dear friend, I am growing. And I pray you are growing too. Since God's love and wisdom exceed infinity; your growth is limited only by the size of your appetite.

Should the final section of this book strain your imagination a bit, read it again after you've whipped up these delicious desserts. After you have tasted them yourself.

It's time for the desserts.

DESSERTS

Desserts...ah, sweet, sweet, desserts. How I've longed to share these with you. Yet, all things must be done DECENTLY AND IN ORDER. God knows we could never taste the beauty of this last course without first eating our basics.

Now you know the importance of accepting Christ as your personal Savior. You know how to receive and hear the Holy Spirit. Next, you'll want to see how this knowledge works in your life.

That's what the desserts are. They are God's knowledge put to use in everyday situations. They are seeing the relevance of your all-powerful Creator in everything around you.

Come, walk with me. Let me lead you through a demonstration of your first dessert. I call it:

RELEVANCE

Let's walk out to the patio. It's cooler there. We can relax and laugh and praise God for the flowers, trees, clouds, and buzzards.

Yes, I said buzzards. We'll get back to them later. But for now, just notice how the patio sets the necessary atmosphere for this dessert.

God saved this delightful patio for me until I could retire from my job in the city and return to my country home. Won't you sit in the yellow swing here under the trees? My dear husband hung it here just for me. So I painted it his favorite color; the color of happiness.

Give yourself a push; lean back and relax. Can you feel the freedom of your childhood...when you use to swing? Look at the brilliant blues in the sky and the pattern of white clouds. No mortal could design that. I wonder who did? Yes, you know...God did! And He did it for you. See how much He loves you?

Close your eyes and listen. The spring fed river in front of us is flowing across a rustic dam. There's peace in its music...peace in the quietness surrounding you. Can you smell the coolness from the waters swishing and swirling across the rocks; washing them whiter and smoother, molding them each to the other?

Relax...take a deep breath, then let it out slowly. Quietly inhale this refreshing symphony. Imagine cool water gently massaging all tension from your neck, shoulders, on down to your toes. Sense a healing of old hurts and worries as they slough off and journey on down the river. All is free...all is cool. A cleansing lightness pervades your body, mind, and soul.

Open your eyes now to the majestic cypress trees bordering the river. What a lesson they teach! Unlike the scrubby mesquite living on rocky ground away from God's ever flowing river. The towering cypress points to the infinity of God above, while mirroring His depth in the river below.

Feel the thick carpet grass beneath your feet. It was full of thistles and briars until God allowed me to share in His creation, by watering it.

The rock wall surrounding the patio? God let me help there, too. I didn't know I had the ability, but He made it easy. Providing natural elements of rock and sand from the gravel bar below the dam; we built this wall.

A breeze is coming up. It feels like angel breath, doesn't it? Soft and gentle and cool, it wisps across your face and caresses your body.

Do you hear that little bird saying, "Pretty, Pret-ty, Pret-ty"? You believe him, too, as you feel yourself sliding into the pattern of God's beautiful nature.

This isn't fantasy dear friend; this is life...life the way God meant it to be. Life abundant, as the Holy Spirit opens your eyes, ears, and thoughts, increasing your awareness of God's love constantly being put to use.

You start to ask me something...but I stop you.

Ssh! If you're very quiet and stop the swing for a minute, you can see another of God's wonders. Look across the river, near that big tree to your right. There's a doe with her fawn. They're edging toward the water. Let's thank God for her presence and the many lessons she teaches through her gentle spirit. Isn't she beautiful? How willingly she protects her mate and young; preceding them into the clearing and signaling when all is safe. Never demanding her own rights; she isn't even aware of her extreme beauty.

"Oh Gwen," you say. "This is truly lovely. I've tasted the dessert of nature before, but never with this much flavor."

Only the Holy Spirit prepares desserts like this. His special ingredient of RELEVANCE makes the difference between an average dessert and one of abundant delights. Only He can turn a dessert into a miracle.

When the Lord was encouraging me to leave the city and return to our place in the country, I claimed His promise in Isaiah 55:12-13.

> "You will live in joy and peace. The mountains and hills, the trees of the field___ all the world around you will rejoice. Where once were thorns, fir trees will grow: where briars grew, the myrtle trees will sprout up. This miracle will make the Lord's name very great and be an everlasting sign of God's power and love."

Since we're still outside, perhaps I can answer the question you've been trying to ask. It's time for your dessert of:

BUZZARD PIE

"Ugh!," you say. You think you'll pass on this dish? I would too if it tasted like its name. But I think you'll enjoy the message. Maybe you'll see why I consider it dessert.

Several encounters with this magnificent bird brought about my fascination of them.

The first encounter involved Red, our buzzard-chasing Doberman Pinscher. Living in the country, it wasn't unusual to see buzzards circling from time to time. However, it did seem unusual that our dog thought she could catch one. It became a family joke. When we saw buzzards circling, we'd all yell, "Buzzard, Red...buzzard" and the chase was on. Never let it be said that Red didn't have high hopes. Especially the day, so intently scanning the sky, she ran into a tree.

Red proved something to me the day she delivered three dead buzzards to my back door. I'm not sure what. Either, "persistence pays off" or "dogs really can fly."

No, I didn't cook the buzzards.

My second encounter, I venture to say, has not been witnessed by many people. It is rather unique.

Invited to explore a 'buzzard's nest', I assumed it would be in a tree. Wrong! When Richard, the neighboring rancher drove his pick-up to the base of a cliff and stopped, we all clambered out. Richard's wife Diane, my husband Gayle, and I looked puzzled.

"There it is," Richard said, pointing to an opening near the top of the cliff.

Queazy, considering the recent reports of mountain lions in the vicinity, we began climbing over the rocks, close behind Richard. Nearing the opening, which we now saw was a cave, a familiar odor begged for definition.

As the odor grew stronger, I knew what it was. The smell of our chicken yard when I was a child.

Sure enough, squinting into the dark interior, we saw what resembled a small chicken yard. The smell confirmed its inhabitants. And the inhabitants were home; the baby buzzards.

Surprised enough by seeing baby buzzards in their natural environment (I wouldn't call it a nest), the real shocker was their color. They were white!

Now, you know buzzards are black. But, did you know they are born white?

It was fun seeing the babies. Personally, I was relieved their mom wasn't home. The thought of meeting a full grown buzzard face to face was incentive enough for me to scamper out the cave and down the cliff.

Although I laughed when Red chased the buzzards and I had been a visitor in their home, I wasn't ready to accept them as friends.

That changed, the day I was driving the usual forty miles to work in Uvalde. I had to slow down while five buzzards left their meal on the road to let me pass. As they retreated and waited patiently until I was gone, I wondered what possible reason God had for creating these repulsive black birds. People usually think of them as ugly and rather nasty; eating only decaying matter, oblivious to the possibility of disease.

Attempting to understand God's wisdom, I thought I could hear Him say, "Gwen, don't be so quick to judge. These buzzards are my Clean-Up Committee. When drivers run over deer, rabbits, or armadillos and neglect the mess, I've made plans to pick up after them. How could you enjoy your drive to work each morning if you had to look at that? I want you to see the beauty of our world."

Praise the Lord for buzzards. Thanks, Lord!

Accepting the buzzards now as a definite plan of God, I looked past my 'not so pleasant' first impression and found other productive qualities.

Fascinated by the buzzard's built-in immune system, I wondered if scientists could explore this phenomena and make use of it in the medical profession. Even many other animals can't eat what the buzzard eats without poisoning their system.

There are times we too must do some pretty dirty work. When this happens, God gives us 'spiritual immunity.' He protects us from contamination in our environment.

Even the Bible seemed to speak to me of buzzards. As I read I Corinthians 4: 12-13, I could picture a group of them gathered around a meal, discussing their plight. (Although this scripture is definitely not referring to buzzards, it's a fun way to look at it.)

> *"We have worked wearily with out hands to*
> *Earn our living.*
> *We have blessed those who cursed us.*
> *We have been patient with those who have*
> *Injured us.*
> *We have replied quietly when evil things have*
> *Been said against us.*
> *Yet, right up to the present moment, we are like*
> *Dirt under foot, like garbage."*

Then, I could almost see the wisest old buzzard in the group straighten his shoulders, lift his head high and walk forward. I recognized his direct words as a summation of my lesson from the buzzards.

"I DO WHAT I LIKE AND I LIKE WHAT I DO."

Not only is the buzzard qualified for his job, but he enjoys doing it. If you have found the job God created you for, using your special talents, you too are enjoying and prospering in your work.

BUZZARDS AND TRASH CANS

Now that you've read the ingredients of Buzzard Pie...get to cooking. Here's how: Always have *physical* and *spiritual* trash cans handy. Get rid of all kinds of trash. Who needs it? If buzzards can do their part, so can you. When trash cans are available, you'll put the trash where it belongs. Shoving it around or dumping it on someone else is not the answer. The trash can is! Keep your home and conscience clean. Then you can say as does the buzzard,

**"I DO WHAT I LIKE
AND
I LIKE WHAT I DO!"**

MORE DESSERTS

I see the sun is getting lower. Shall we return to the house? There are stacks of desserts there you haven't seen; much less tasted.

You're looking at your watch. You're right. It is time for you to go.

How sad! This time was inevitable because with God, there's always SOMETHING MORE. Something new, we want to taste and share.

However, as you leave, please take the rest of my simple recipes with you. Some are desserts, some are meat and bread, and some will just fill that empty spot when you don't know what you are hungry for.

Cut them from the back of this book. Place one daily on a small easel in your kitchen. Put them to use. Grow in the Lord. Sorry, I wasn't able to put these in the book as I had planned, but you can order them from me over my web page

www.angelfoodblessings.com

or through the mail at:

Angel Food Blessings
HC 69 - Box 282
Sabinal, Texas 78881.

I watch you now, going down my steps and onto the sidewalk. A load of recipes in your arms and a smile on your face; you turn and wave goodbye.

"Goodbye dear friend," I think. "I can hardly wait for our next meeting. I know you are serious about your cooking. Oh, what joy awaits you. When you return, you will be doing all the talking. You will have so many new and wonderful recipes to share. Recipes God has created 'just for you.'"

Then I turn to God...a burden lifted, and say, "In my jumbled, mixed up way, Lord, I've tried to carry out your command in Isaiah 30:8-9 (LBP)."

> *"Now go and write down this word of mine...*
> *For if you don't write it, they will claim*
> *I never warned them. 'Oh, no,', they'll say,*
> *'You never told us that.'"*

Now, I've told what I know, Lord. You'll do the rest.

ANGEL FOOD

```
THANK YOU JESUS
      FOR
YOUR ANGEL FOOD!
```